The Mandate

How good people struggle with bad mandates,
and what to do about it

Bas van Heel

Uitgeverij Helium

2018

The Mandate

How good people struggle with bad mandates, and what to do about it

Author:	Bas van Heel
Illustrations:	CartoonStock.com, iStock.com
Proofreading:	Proof-Reading-Service.com, UK
Graphic Design:	Helium, grafische vormgeving, NL
Publisher:	Uitgeverij Helium, NL

ISBN: **978 90 79841 09 7**

NUR: 801

Keywords: management, organisation, mandate, manual, checklist, examples

This is not a work of fiction. But I have simplified and dressed up the examples for the sake of clarity, and changed the names of the lead characters.

© Uitgeverij Helium, Utrecht | 6/2018

Available from Amazon.

info@uitgeverijhelium.nl

Uitgeverij Helium

Contents

Introduction

One year ago you have accepted a great and challenging assignment.
Without too much due diligence you have accepted it.
Now you are reflecting if the endeavour is on track and if your input is sustainable.
Some of you are capable (in your context) to deliver the required change/growth/innovation/transformation by just 'being there' and stimulating the right people doing the right thing. On the other end of the spectrum you may be struggling, overwhelmed by complexity and lack of support, while your energy levels are evaporating.

Most people across this spectrum would benefit from assessing their mandate, to become more effective, or even just to survive.
This manual describes what is a mandate, provides a framework and it's key elements, and how to mitigate limitations in suboptimal mandates.
It also describes why we find it hard to make mandates explicit, and how to deal with that hurdle.
Various examples illustrate the framework.

This manual can be used to check an existing mandate, ideally before it becomes urgent, or help build a new one.

Testing this manual I have received positive feedback but also some criticism:

"I recognise many issues that were not ideal in my past jobs, but not sure if applying this manual would have fixed them all."
I don't pretend applying this checklist/manual will help you to get a perfect mandate, that would be naïve. If this manual would just help you to overcome the hurdle to discuss your mandate with your mandate provider, then most likely some of the issues can get addressed.

"It is complete, but it is too much: 5 things to worry about, broken down into 12 elements."
This is not a book to read to become inspired with a new concept. It is a manual. So read some of the stories, not necessarily the whole book. And use the 12 element-check list to assess your mandate.

I trust you can use this manual to improve your mandate, even by just putting it on your mandate provider's desk.

1

Example case: how good people struggle with a bad mandate

Frank asked me to help him think through the issues he had at work. He was hired 4 months ago by the CEO as programme manager for a hospital chain improvement programme in Germany. The objective was to ensure the improvement projects that were already defined would be executed.

After 2 discussions with Frank, the following became clear:
- The CEO had made a full commitment to the shareholders and one of the related insurance companies
- The objective was nothing short of a transformation with a significant impact on quality and profit
- The projects were mostly in the idea phase without clear action plans and benefits
- The people that were to execute these projects (doctors) had no time as they needed to treat patients
- The broader set of people involved in each project was not (yet) convinced on each project
- The insurance company was funding the transformation programme as an example programme for other hospital chains
- A few project managers were supporting the programme, but were being paid by the insurance company. They ensured that the hospital did what the insurance company wanted to test, and did not help the programme manager execute the programme
- The programme manager only had one inexperienced person to help him, and no budget

We devised three options to deal with this situation:
1. The bottom up creation of a coalition of the willing (the doctors) so that their very limited spare time can be used to create traction on the projects that really interest them (related to quality)
2. Use your own time and the support person to get 1 project fully on track, then work on the next, etc.
3. Confront the CEO with the way we see the situation, and try to get a proper programme organisation and mandate

Frank had already done option 1 and was getting beyond tired, with signs of burnout surfacing. Frank had started to try option 2 but realised that this would be much too slow. So he talked with the CEO. The CEO said: "I hired you to get the programme on track, so you need to fix this. That is your role."

Continuing to suggest improvements about the mandate resulted in Frank getting fired. He now happily works somewhere else with a clear mandate.

"What are you still doing here? I told you what to do, go and do it!"

2 Definition: what is a mandate?

The word mandate is derived from the Latin word 'mandare': to commission, order, commend. Interestingly enough, on Wikipedia, the concept of a mandate has many meanings but not the one used in management. _https://en.wikipedia.org/wiki/Mandate_

Also, when googling for the term mandate, the concept is most often used in politics: a mandate is provided by the voters for a politicians' next term in office. However, the concept of a mandate as defined in chapter 3 is applicable much more broadly, although often not addressed in such an explicit way.

For this booklet, we will use this definition: A deal between a mandate provider and mandate taker, providing a set of power/resources to achieve a specific objective.

In this manual, we focus on situations in management. In management, there are many situations with different mandate challenges:
- Supervisory board/management board: between the chairman and the CEO
- Cooperative: between the members and the CEO
- Programme manager: between the programme owner and programme manager
- Project manager: between the project owner and project manager
- Consultant: between the client and the consultant

So far, I have not seen significant differences between these various situations with respect to the mandate issue, so I will describe just one approach, and apply it across various examples.

In the examples we show situations within one company, with the mandate provider being more senior than the mandate taker. Lateral deals (even outside one company) could also probably benefit from this manual, but they have not been explored here.

3 The role of the mandate: when and why is it important?

When is it important?

If you

- head a company/department,
- and have a clear achievable objective,
- and are not dependent on other players/departments,
- and are not confronted with significant change,

then usually mandates are reasonably clear.

But in our globalising, technology-driven economy, very often the main value is created by working across departments/teams and companies. Organising according to 'agile' principles does not resolve this complexity, it actually requires an even clearer mandate for each team.

In that case, success depends on alignment across the various functional/company borders. Very often, the people that are expected to build/implement the new solution/value proposition are provided with a compelling objective but not with the required means and power. I have met many people in such a situation getting frustrated (and the objective not materialising), possibly for the wrong reason.

Sometimes companies try to resolve these complexities by reorganising. This often absorbs all energy for 1-2 years, usually resulting in the new organisation having the same amount of complexity, just in different areas. It can be better to address this complexity by addressing the complexity of a specific endeavour by a good mandate, making the complexity issue smaller rather than bigger.

If you are not sure (as provider or taker) if the situation requires a mandate, ask yourself the following questions about the specific objective

- Is it a significant change, versus the normal operating model?
- Does it involve significant cross-functional change?
- Is it a non-linear initiative with unpredictable events?
- Will the associated organisational complexity still exist beyond the start-up phase of the initiative?

If two or three questions are answered with a 'Yes', then you need a mandate. Two other ways to check this are:

- Asking the mandate taker; they often sense if this will work without any additional mandate
- Going through the checklist in the following chapters; if nothing raises an eyebrow than you may be OK without a mandate

Why is it important?

If a particular initiative requires a mandate, this should ideally be done right at the start. The elements that were already clear won't take much time. You can then focus on the elements that are tricky, and maximise the chance of success. Also, it provides a framework and process for regular updates.

If the mandate is not discussed early on, mostly it gets discussed when things are not going well. This means the objective is unlikely to be met, credibility could be impacted and fixing a mandate could become more difficult than at the start.

So, let us explore the perspective of the mandate provider, and the mandate taker, using various examples, and distil a framework on how to understand and improve a typical mandate.

4 How it links to other frameworks

If we look at related frameworks, we do see overlap with the concept of a mandate. But these frameworks miss certain elements:

Project management

A very good framework for project management is Prince2 (_https://en.wikipedia. org/wiki/PRINCE2_), it well describes the mechanics of good project management. I have seen such an approach at work several times, but sometimes it fails to deliver results. A well-trained project manager manages all the steps (stage gates). But often the overall objective is not achieved. Frequently, this is caused by the lack of a good understanding of the content, due to the belief that a solid project approach will take care of everything. Furthermore, it assumes the project controls all the required resources. This is where the concept of the mandate comes in. Also, many mandate situations are more complex than a single project, and thinking in terms of a mandate is more effective before detailing the elements of a good project.

Responsibility models

Many models exist to determine programme/project responsibilities. For example, RACI (_https://en.wikipedia.org/wiki/Responsibility_assignment_matrix_). The problem with these models is that they do not describe the role of the mandate provider.

Change management

The best framework for change management I know is provided by John Kotter (_https://en.wikipedia.org/wiki/John_Kotter_). It describes the 8 steps to leading change. This gets us closer to the concept of a mandate. Step two (creating the guiding coalition) includes the question of whether there 'are enough key players on board so that those left out cannot easily block progress?' And step 5 (empowering broad based action) talks about eliminating barriers, adapting systems and structures that are in the way, and encouraging risks. But his change manual is much broader than a simple mandate between a mandate provider and taker.

Neither of these frameworks describes the dynamics of the dialogue between the mandate provider and the mandate taker.

5 Elements of a good mandate and how to mitigate gaps

For this manual, we define 4 roles:

- Stakeholders: customers, shareholders, employees, external stakeholders
- Provider: the person providing the mandate
- Taker: the person taking the mandate
- Resources: the resources required to succeed

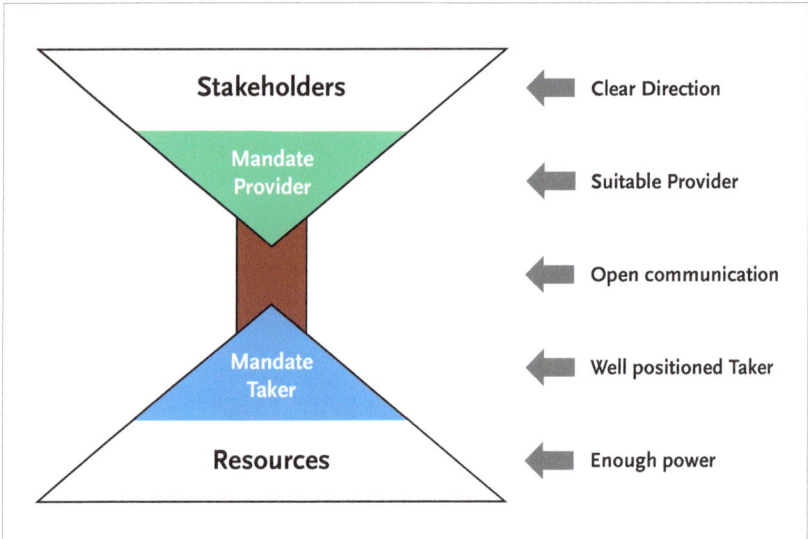

Roles and elements of a good mandate

The 12 elements of a good mandate can be grouped into five types:

Clear direction
1. A clear objective with enough autonomy
2. A clear strategy/approach
3. A clear timeline
4. Alignment on the mandate across all stakeholders
5. Suitable guardrails

A suitable mandate provider
6. A suitable mandate provider

A well-positioned mandate taker
7. A suitable mandate taker
8. Suitable reward
9. Sense of belonging

Enough power over resources
10. Sufficient directly controllable resources
11. Sufficient power over critical, not directly controllable, actors

Open communication between the mandate provider and taker
12. Open communication between mandate taker and provider to adjust the mandate

In the rest of this chapter, these elements are described as the ideal situation.

However, it does not make sense to aim for the perfect mandate. By the time it is built, the opportunity will have evaporated. But at least make the limitations explicit, and find sufficient mitigating measures. So, for each element a few examples of mitigation are listed, but be creative in devising your own.

Clear Direction

1. *A clear objective with enough autonomy*
   - Ideally frame the objective as a 'what', not as a 'how', to ensure the mandate taker has enough autonomy to think out of the box to find the best route/solution to achieving the objective

   Mitigation:
   - Sometimes the precise ultimate objective is not yet clear. Then define an intermediate objective, and arrange to adjust over time
   - Sometimes the autonomy/out of the box options are hard to sell. Some progress (e.g. on diagnosis, lateral examples) may be needed to earn the right to advance in a more creative way
   - If the mandate is very weak, (temporarily) downscale the objective: e.g. from building a completely new cross-company business development process to acquiring 1-2 new customers in a better way

2. *A clear strategy/approach*
   - Linked to the overall company mission/strategy
   - Based on a good understanding of the relevant issues, and a proper change & communication approach

   Mitigation:
   - If you insist on starting to design/implement based on (bad) assumptions, make explicit that this is a trial, while, in parallel, build the foundation

3. *A clear timeline*
   - Use milestones for major events, avoid drawing project (micro) management into the mandate
   - Often a mandate is for a specific activity, so clarify when (and how) this activity will end, and the result will be transferred to the line organisation

   Mitigation:
   - If it is too early to establish clear milestones, establish initial high level milestones, and communicate when you will detail them

4. *Alignment on the mandate across all stakeholders*
   - It is often hard for the mandate taker to create internal & external stakeholder alignment by himself
   - Stakeholder management is not about writing your plan and sharing it with the stakeholders, in some situations the strategy/approach is 80% about stakeholder management, so their perspective needs to be incorporated as an integral element of the strategy

   Mitigation:
   - If the mandate provider has not done this (sufficiently), then it becomes an explicit part of the mandate to build the required stakeholder alignment, likely requiring the help of the mandate provider
   - If the mandate taker is new to the organisation, provide an in-company mentor to help them navigate the organisation
   - Build an (informal) set of people that will benefit from the mandate taker's work, to start developing traction/credibility

5. *Suitable guardrails*
   - Agree what are the most critical risks and how to track them e.g. monitor team engagement/overload or customer satisfaction/disruption

   Mitigation:
   - If explicitly tracking these risks is not feasible, be more creative. Otherwise ensure an (informal) process is in place (e.g. a few regular one-on-one conversations)

A suitable mandate provider

6. *A suitable mandate provider*
   - There is a balance between power and available time: the more senior the mandate provider, the greater is the power over all relevant resources, but there is less time to spend on the endeavour
   - Obviously, the mandate provider also needs to be very interested in and capable on the subject

   Mitigation:
   - In case they have sufficient power, they need to mobilise others and find a way to get them on board
   - In case they have insufficient time, they may need to involve a substitute that has more time, and a good feel for the subject, and easy access to the mandate provider
   - The power/time balance is more important than content knowledge (the mandate taker can resolve that), but a lack of interest is very hard to compensate for

A well-positioned mandate taker

7. *A suitable mandate taker*
   - Some people say that with a good mandate taker you do not need a strong mandate. I do not agree, but a suitable mandate taker is obviously critical

   Mitigation:
   - Compensate for missing capabilities through the capabilities of other team members

8. *Suitable reward*
   - Most mandates are about larger/longer activities, so it is relevant to talk about a reward in terms of a promotion or any other significant reward that is prominent in the mind of the mandate taker
   - Avoid replacing intrinsic motivation (mandate taker is passionate about the objective) with just external motivation (e.g. money), so arrange for colleagues to (genuinely) express their appreciation

   Mitigation:
   - If the priority needs of the mandate taker cannot be satisfied, be creative in trying to satisfy other needs, without overpromising

9. *Sense of belonging*
    - Sometimes the objective is such that the mandate taker does not have many peers. The risk is that the mandate taker becomes isolated. This is not sustainable

    Mitigation:
    - If not obvious how to do this with direct colleagues, create a group of likeminded people that provide a sense of belonging/moral support. This can also be outside the company

Enough power over resources

10. *Sufficient directly controllable resources*
    - Enough latitude to pick their own team
    - Enough budget to build the right capacity/capability from internal/external sources

    Mitigation:
    - Often a chicken and egg problem: first show results then resources will follow. Build a smart roadmap so early results can encourage the stepping up of resources

11. *Sufficient power over critical, not directly controllable, actors*
    - As mentioned at the start, most high impact change programmes are multifunctional, and the mandate taker rarely has direct control over all the relevant resources, so the mandate provider needs to arrange for enough power over all required resources, including access to resources outside the company (e.g. customers, suppliers)
    - Sometimes the mandate provider does not have this power herself. In that case, the objectives need to be adjusted, and/or a more senior manager needs to become part of the initiative

    Mitigation:
    - Avoid making it bigger (e.g. by linking it to a forthcoming reorganisation). A blanket power-mandate is rarely realistic
    - Engineer specific elements of power related to specific steps e.g. for the mandate provider, by making minor agreements with other functions, or for the taker, by focussing on people who will quickly benefit

Open communication between the mandate provider and taker

12. *Open communication between mandate taker and provider to adjust the mandate*
    - This is the most critical element, to which we dedicate the whole next chapter. It ensures the other elements can be discussed from the start and adjusted along the way, when the situation changes.
    - The mandate taker often has the best view on the critical success factors, so the mandate taker needs to ensure that he sets (most of) the agenda for the provider/taker meeting

    Mitigation:
    - If a mandate provider does not have enough time, she needs to provide a delegate with enough insight and power
    - A mandate provider with insufficient power himself needs to be clear about it and adjust the objectives/approach accordingly

Other elements
The above list describes the most common and important elements. To avoid making an impractically long list, we need to check for other elements in order to identity any situation-specific issues e.g. I learnt of one situation where someone was blocked from taking a mandate due to his non-compete clause, and the programme set-up had to be adjusted, with some impact on the objective.

The most important element of a good mandate: open communication between mandate provider and taker

6 Why not talk about the mandate?

Some people may say the list of elements of a good mandate in the previous chapter is common sense. I certainly hope so. But then why does it still go wrong so often? I learnt that both the mandate provider and the taker often hesitate to explicitly talk about the mandate, and thus the discussion never happens, or too superficially, or only when things are visibly not going well.

In this chapter, I list the reasons I have heard/distilled for the mandate provider and taker not talking about the mandate and how to address them.

Reasons for mandate providers not to talk about the mandate

Not realising the need (in time)
- Not sure this is a mandate situation, she is just doing her job
- Unclear when the initiative is changing from a few subtle discussions into a full programme, so not realising when this requires a mandate

Underestimating the need
- Isn't it obvious what needs to be done?
- Good people don't need a mandate: we appoint the best person, she will fix it

Unable to limit/fence-off uncertainties in the broader context
- We are not sure yet about the new idea so we cannot provide a solid mandate
- The main actors are not yet sold on the idea, so we first need proof that it works
- The organisation is not stable (we are reorganising, or in a merger, ...), so we cannot yet provide a good mandate
- I am glad he took the job, not sure about the outcome, let us see how far he gets

Unwilling to admit own limitations
- I don't even have the power myself to provide the elements of the mandate he is/would be asking for and I feel hesitant to make that explicit
- There is too much organisational complexity above/around me, and I don't want to confuse him by talking about that

Unwilling to spend power

- The objective is not important enough to me (e.g. because it is a small part in a larger plan) to spend time/resources/power on it
- I have just been asked to be the mandate provider for this objective, as people thought I was most suitable. But it has no link to my own objectives, so I am not going to expend effort on it
- I cannot afford to expend real resources or power. But I don't want to make that explicit as it will demotivate the taker

Surprisingly, the initiative to talk about a good mandate often comes from the mandate taker. It sometimes seems the mandate provider has the illusion that it is effective to push the mandate taker into saying yes to the objective without checking the mandate. Realise that the mandate taker may hesitate to ask for a better mandate, and initiate the discussion yourself.

Also, ideally, don't translate your own uncertainties into a bad mandate. If the initiative fails, you will never know if it was a bad idea or a bad mandate.

Some ways to deal with the uncertainties

- Never delay a discussion about the mandate. Don't wait until it becomes necessary. Then the delay has invariably caused damage already. Better to do it at the start and address the various uncertainties explicitly
- Break it down into smaller parts, for instance:
  - First, mandate the diagnosis phase
  - Reduce the scope
  - Downsize the deliverables to match the resources/power
- Make the uncertainties explicit and regularly adjust the mandate according to the changing context.
- When the uncertainties are larger, comfort the taker by saying that you will support him during this unpredictable journey (and then deliver)

Reasons for the mandate taker not to talk about the mandate

Not realising the need (in time)
- Just doing my job, not realising the need for a mandate
- We will take it as it comes
- We have no time to organise for a strong mandate
- Not realising that this key meeting where we share our ambition /the objective is the best/only/last time to ask for a strong mandate. People will remember the deliverable but will not realise you have not yet asked for the matching resources/power
- If I detail all the steps (I have seen them with a few hundred actions) with a name and deadline, and then manage against these, then I will be sure to succeed

Insecurity
- I am new here so I cannot ask for a strong mandate
- Asking for a strong mandate feels like weakness
- Limited alternative job prospects, so wary of asking for a better mandate
- If I ask about resources and power then the objective (that seems hard to deliver) also will be made explicit, so it is better to keep it vague

Overconfident
- I am best equipped to do this part of the job, so I will do it myself (then often drowning in it)
- If they don't want to help me, I will do it myself
- If there is no budget, I will do it myself
- Accepting scope creep
- Accepting overly ambitious goals

Naive
- Having an implicit dream about the ideal organisation/context, and working as if that context will materialise soon

Better deal with it up-front

Ideally, do a due diligence (use the checklist) before you accept an (implicit) mandate, so you can discuss the parameters as part of accepting it.
Even if this has not been done, most mandate takers quickly realise they lack

certain elements in their mandate. Don't push away your good gut feeling that something is not right. Make an explicit trade-off between the risks/effort/delay of asking for a better mandate versus risking the success of the project, or even worse, your health.

Invariably, it is better to talk about it than not. It is more about the tone/approach of the discussion, and realising some of the hesitations/limitations of the mandate provider.

Having had the discussion at the start also establishes the framework and facilitates coming back to it.

If you find it hard to open the discussion, consider sharing this manual with them.

Death-trap between the mandate provider and taker

Sometimes the hesitation to talk about the mandate is shared by the provider and taker, and an implicit agreement arises not to discuss the mandate explicitly.

"So we agree to sweep my mandate under your carpet?"

7

Analysing the example *(Text of chapter 1, copied for your convenience)*

Frank asked me to help him think through the issues he had at work. He was hired 4 months ago by the CEO as programme manager for a hospital chain improvement programme in Germany. The objective was to ensure the improvement projects that were already defined would be executed.

After 2 discussions with Frank, the following became clear:
- The CEO had made a full commitment to the shareholders and one of the related insurance companies
- The objective was nothing short of a transformation with a significant impact on quality and profit
- The projects were mostly in the idea phase without clear action plans and benefits
- The people that were to execute these projects (doctors) had no time as they needed to treat patients
- The broader set of people involved in each project was not (yet) convinced on each project
- The insurance company was funding the transformation programme as an example programme for other hospital chains
- A few project managers were supporting the programme, but were being paid by the insurance company. They ensured that the hospital did what the insurance company wanted to test, and did not help the programme manager execute the programme
- The programme manager only had one inexperienced person to help him, and no budget

We devised three options to deal with this situation:
1. The bottom up creation of a coalition of the willing (the doctors) so that their very limited spare time can be used to create traction on the projects that really interest them (related to quality)
2. Use your own time and the support person to get 1 project fully on track, then work on the next, etc.
3. Confront the CEO with the way we see the situation, and try to get a proper programme organisation and mandate

Frank had already done option 1 and was getting beyond tired, with signs of burnout surfacing. Frank had started to try option 2 but realised that this would be much too slow. So he talked with the CEO. The CEO said: "I hired you to get the programme on track, so you need to fix this. That is your role." Continuing to suggest improvements about the mandate resulted in Frank getting fired. He now happily works somewhere else with a clear mandate.

Analysis of the example case
(10 is good, 1 is bad)

	Element	Score	Comment
Clear direction			
1	Clear objective & autonomy	10	Clear objective: ensure the projects are executed; Enough autonomy
2	Clear strategy/approach	3	Most project were in the ideas stage, and not yet analysed
3	A clear timeline	5	Clear that the projects needed to gain traction but no timeline was yet agreed
4	Alignment with stakeholders	5	The insurance company was happy with it, but not the doctors
5	Suitable guardrails	3	No guardrail on personal sustainability
Suitable mandate provider			
6	Suitable mandate provider	8	CEO
Well positioned mandate taker			
7	A suitable mandate taker	6	Good experience with programmes, lack of experience in hospitals and related difficult stakeholder issues
8	Suitable reward	6	Compensation was fine, future role not clear
9	Sense of belonging	3	Not embedded in (mainstream) team
Enough Power			
10	Sufficient directly controllable resources	1	No budget, only 1 FTE; Project managers provided were checking, not helping Frank
11	Sufficient power over not directly controllable actors	1	No power over doctors, who were not given the time or incentives to progress the projects
Open communication			
12	Open communication between provider & taker	3	Just do it. Update meetings did not yield improvement of mandate

Reasons for the mandate provider not to talk about the mandate:
The main actors are not yet sold on the idea, so we first need proof that it works
Good people don't need a mandate: we appoint the best person, he will fix it
Not sure this is a mandate situation, he is just doing his job

Reasons for the mandate taker not to talk about the mandate:
I am new here so I cannot ask for a strong mandate
Asking for a strong mandate feels like weakness
Not sure this is a mandate situation, I am just doing my job

8 More examples

8.1 The global sector leader in a professional service provider

Anita was asked to start a project going after a new sector on a global basis. During the kick-off, 6 partners from 6 countries were present. Some said this sector did not buy any consulting work, some said the sector was dominated by the main competitor. Some said both. This did not make sense but Anita interpreted this as meaning that these partners had better/easier opportunities. The sector was in turmoil and Anita saw good potential. Being of the entrepreneurial type, she put aside the comments from the kick-off and got to work. She got a budget, put a team together, listed the target clients, and started to write a report about the sector as an entry ticket.

To everyone's surprise, it actually went quite well. Slowly, more and more clients from the original hit-list were served. On the other hand, Anita was not too happy about how the organisation was treating her. Her line manager was in Spain, her HR boss in Germany, and her office was in Belgium. As long as the revenues materialised, this fragmented reporting line gave her close to unlimited freedom. But the HR function started to make demands that were at odds with the business, and it took 5 years longer than promised to provide the rewards linked to what she achieved. Also, having started as a project, the business was integrated into a larger sector team. This was a good idea to create a sense of belonging, but the larger sector team had no power to support Anita, and the linkages were too weak to provide any real synergy, and, as a result, the sense of belonging did not materialise. In spite of these issues, Anita carried on, motivated by the cooperation with the many client teams she had helped to shape.

Eventually, the number of projects increased to such an extent that Anita needed more help than the two people that supported her could provide. She spent 3 years exploring and pushing for options to extend the team. All ideas were encouraged, but killed once formalised. The whole endeavour became more of a burden than a source of energy and pride, so Anita left.

Analysis

(The arrow in the score-column indicating the change over the years)

	Element	Score	Comment
Clear direction			
1	Clear objective & autonomy	10	Clear objective: explore new sector; Full autonomy
2	Clear strategy/approach	7>10	The client target list was made in week 1, content developed quickly and deepened over the years
3	A clear timeline	10	Check if it can work in 3 years; If yes, then grow further
4	Alignment with stakeholders	2	Very limited interest from the partners in the countries that mattered
5	Suitable guardrails	4	No guardrail on personal sustainability
Suitable mandate provider			
6	Suitable mandate provider	3>4	The mandate providers had no power over critical resources
Well positioned mandate taker			
7	A suitable mandate taker	7	Good consultant, entrepreneurial spirit, but lacking patience and a constraint on accepting too much work
8	Suitable reward	3	Complete mismatch between promised and delivered reward in terms of pay, promotion and respect
9	Sense of belonging	3	Very late and too limited integration into mainstream line management
Enough Power			
10	Sufficient directly controllable resources	4>1	Initial budget, but was stopped when the business grew; No mandate for team extension
11	Sufficient power over not directly controllable actors	1>4	Initially Anita had to create traction herself, the integration into a larger sector provided some help
Open communication			
12	Open communication between provider & taker	1>5	Initially on her own; Later part of a larger sector, but not really embedded, without power

Reasons for the mandate provider not to talk about the mandate:
Did not have any power over the teams in the country that would have to go after the target clients. So the mandate was: just go and do it
Did not have any power over resources to support Anita, but initially indicated he did, so left Anita in a useless chase for team resources

Reasons for the mandate taker not to talk about the mandate:
Anita's enthusiasm for building a new business stopped her from pressing for a better mandate on resources. She would have found earlier they would not be realistic
The same drive prevented her from just aiming for a lower target, given no help was available. This could have kept her energy up, but unclear if this 'rescaling' would have motivated her

8.2 The European marketing team

Pierre just started at a global industrial company in a European marketing function. The company had moved its European marketing function from England to France, and was losing some of its people, so was hiring to fill the gaps. Also, it was about to be taken over by another company so everybody was insecure about their jobs. A consultant had prepared a 1 year plan to improve the marketing function in Europe. Pierre and I discussed how to best function in his new role during 2 periods:

Just starting: what to do?
A few months after having started, Pierre had still not been introduced to the broader company with a clear role. Just go and talk to everybody. The fluid context of the organisation resulted in his boss and his superiors functioning in a wait and see mode. Not ideal when you have a 1 year contract with an option to turn this into a fixed contract based on performance. The positive side was that he could influence his role and his boss was open to any idea/ discussion. Pierre decided to go for a role where he could show impact in a year and which had limited overlap with the acquiring company to avoid becoming redundant during the forthcoming merger. He started to act in this role, and by doing this, induced his boss to communicate that Pierre was focussing on this role for this year.

After half a year: what is next, how to survive?
Pierre was doing the right thing, but got tired of doing too much in an unstable environment. Three issues became clear. Firstly, the plan, as prepared by the consultant, was complete and it was less clear what to do next. Secondly, the many formal/informal stakeholders all had different ideas about priorities. Specifically, the global marketing function had some very strong initiatives (some of which did not fit in the European context), while the locally op- erating companies still had most of the power; the European function was squeezed in the middle. Thirdly, Pierre had focussed on achieving results and had insufficiently managed the relationship with direct/indirect reports and various stakeholders. Given that the short-term results were coming in, Pierre agreed with his boss to spend 2 month making a new plan. He would map out a complete programme as he saw it, and then shop it around to find out which elements carried enough backing from the global/regional/local stakehold- ers, which required fine-tuning, and which would better wait until after the merger. This would result in a plan backed by most stakeholders, and at the same time, allow him to ask about how to improve the cooperating model, to improve the key relationships.
It seems that the open relationship between mandate provider and taker will overcome the many deficiencies in other mandate elements.

Analysis

	Element	Score	Comment
Clear direction			
1	Clear objective & autonomy	3	Not clear objective, started as filling the gaps in the regional organisation, and executing a short-term plan
2	Clear strategy/approach	3	Company goals were clear, but not yet translated to marketing priorities
3	A clear timeline	2	No timeline
4	Alignment with stakeholders	2	Global initiatives and local plans were disconnected and regional function stuck in the middle
5	Suitable guardrails	5	No guardrail on personal sustainability
Suitable mandate provider			
6	Suitable mandate provider	6	Pierre's boss had reasonable power and time
Well positioned mandate taker			
7	A suitable mandate taker	7	Experienced person but not rooted in the company
8	Suitable reward	3	It was not clear what Pierre needed to do to meet his main need: a fixed contract
9	Sense of belonging	3	Not OK in the very fluid organisation
Enough Power			
10	Sufficient directly controllable resources	7	Pierre had various direct reports and could hire a few more
11	Sufficient power over not directly controllable actors	2	Pierre had to build this based on his own credibility
Open communication			
12	Open communication between provider & taker	8	Pierre's boss was open for any discussion and supported Pierre

Reasons for the mandate provider not to talk about the mandate:
The fluid marketing function and the forthcoming merger prevented providing a clear mandate

Reasons for the mandate taker not to talk about the mandate:
Having a 1 year temporary contract made Pierre somewhat hesitant to ask for a better mandate

8.3   The ambitious chairman

The choice of Andreas as the new chairman was a surprise. He was very entrepreneurial and had had some issues before with pioneering outside the comfort zone of his previous organisation. This seemed like my kind of guy, but he had just become chairman of a very large but conservative company with a very diverse portfolio, and a culture of very solid, very deliberate decision-making. Some parts of the portfolio were at risk from the digitisation revolution, but also had several major potential upsides. The people that appointed him must have bold plans. Andreas asked me to help out. We prepared a 2 day vision/strategy session with the main shareholders, supervisory and the managing board members. It went well, and most participants saw the need/opportunity to more fundamentally and more quickly adjust the company strategies, a full transformation. So, Andreas started to initiate changes in the organisation to be able to drive this transformation. But the management board did not agree with the depth and speed of the transformation, and they controlled all the resources. It started to get out of hand when the chairman and CEO started to use the press to communicate about what was best. Later on, the stories in the paper even became very personal. It also became a bit tense for myself when Andreas started to invite journalists to our office, when his CEO did not allow this to happen at his company. Eventually Andres fired the CEO. But the CEO had more friends in the group of shareholders, so shortly after Andreas was also fired.

Years later, most of the transformational ideas were implemented anyway. I don't know if the delay resulted in missed opportunities, or if the more gradual approach achieved the same impact with less stress for everyone involved.

I have not been able to find out who had selected Andreas as chairman, and what the idea behind his appointment was. But it was clear, in hindsight, that Andreas thought he had a much stronger mandate than he actually did.

8.4   The cooperative

Sometimes you are lucky. I was sitting in a bus in Singapore with all the CEO's of the companies I ever wanted to have as a client. One of them told me not to sit next to him, but next to his friend, as he would have more need for our services. He did, a few months later we started a very interesting project. So I had a great time in that bus.

These CEO's were together for a shareholders meeting of a cooperative shared service company. I was invited as I often helped the cooperative. The companies were very large retailers across the globe. Peter, the cooperative's CEO, had asked me to motivate the shareholders to invite more companies to participate in the cooperative to reflect the globalising nature of the market. I was happy to do so as I thought it was the right thing to do for the coopera- tive, and I was happy to help him. We had invited the potential new members and the CEO's of the largest existing members to join a small panel discussion about the changing market structure, and the corresponding logical member- ship extension. The potential new members were very happy to join, and the existing members agreed.
However, this was just a panel discussion and the subsequent full cooperative shareholders meeting stopped the initiative. They first wanted the cooperative to deliver on a major programme. We had helped to put that together, and had commented on the need for a business case for each participant, and a stron- ger overall governance, when our involvement ended. The programme had not yet delivered the required result.

At first glance, this appeared to have to do with:
- The previous CEO of the cooperative, who had not spent enough time on the execution of the programme
- The chairman looking for consensus, more than a coalition of the willing

But at a closer look, it had more to do with the structure of the mandate, as we had anticipated:
- The programme governance was set up such that the cooperative only carried responsibility for delivering the infrastructure, while some mem- bers did not have the capabilities, or market opportunity, or investment priority to utilise this infrastructure
- The set-up depended on network economics, demanding everyone par- ticipate to yield the required benefit
- The CEO's of the member companies did not allow the cooperative to expend real effort connecting to the business units of the members that were supposed to make money on the new infrastructure, to check their real requirements

- The result was that the members blamed the cooperative for not delivering on the network economics, while the cooperative only had a mandate to deliver the infrastructure

Peter, the new CEO, recently asked us to help put it right. Let's see what happens.

This example seems to be representative for cooperatives: the cooperative accepts or assumes objectives it cannot meet without a stronger mandate. The resulting chicken and egg situation (you don't get the required resources/ mandate unless you first prove your added value) often has a bad impact on the relationships. It helps to ask a fresh team to explore the strategy options in depth, including the real required mandate for each option.

8.5   The 50/50 Joint Venture

When we were shown in we saw a large man sitting behind a large desk. He looked like a king receiving his underlings. But Bernhard was a very friendly and smart man. He was the COO of a 50/50 Joint Venture in shared services. His supervisory board had 'suggested' that Bernhard ask us for help. We were to prepare the business plan for a major investment plan. The plan was based on a range of very creative ideas, but we soon found out that adding up all these ideas would cost more than a year of revenues, in a sector that was declining fast. We helped Bernhard and his team to distil the valuable great ideas, and scale down the cost of the lesser ideas. This was fun work, but appeared not to be the real issue. The company was in need of a more structural transformation. The problem was that the two owners did not agree on the direction. It soon became apparent that the original synergy in the shared services between the two owner's companies was evaporating quickly. A 50/50 JV inherently has a very tricky governance model, but once the strategy of the two owners is also diverging, it becomes a nightmare. The two owners had hoped to evade trouble by allowing the company to build its own strategy serving other companies for similar services. However, the market scope for these services was too small to allow the company to become sufficiently independent from the two owners.

This issue became one of those festering underlying problems that gets in the way of any progress: so far, every three years the shared service company has had a new CEO. This new CEO found things did not work well and so changed the fundamental strategy of the company: from a shared service company just serving the two owners to a company serving the general shared services market. The next CEO took a fresh look and switched it back. Etcetera. Now a smart colleague of mine had once found that really profound change in a company may take 6 months per layer to really stick. The company had 6 layers, so a real change would take 3 years. By the time the change had reached the operational level, the new CEO would change direction. This describes an organisation where everybody is moving about at great speed but the organisation does not move. Fortunately, our client, the COO, managed the company in a very pragmatic way and most people just did their job.

Eventually, the JV was dismantled and each JV partner reengineered its services to its own needs. So, everybody was happy. However, 20 years after the start of the journey described here, I learnt that a very small part of the shared services remained. I read in the newspaper that a problem had emerged with its manager: he had a great idea about building the shared service into an independent business, serving other customers.

Thinking back about the 20 year transformation journey of this company, it was interesting to notice how such a fundamental strategic issue has been the root cause of a flawed mandate, causing many common-sense things to be done late or with great difficulty.

8.6   The business development manager

John worked as business development manager in a large insurance company. The company had major ambitions to transform its business model, and was in a merger at the same time. John's role was to grow a particular segment. This segment was to be one of the cornerstones of the new business model, and John was passionate about the segment as well as the future business model. The only snag was that the new business model was not yet clear, let alone implemented. Also, the segment's priority had been translated into targets, but not yet into resource planning. The segment required many different people from various departments to cooperate.

John had asked various times for a clear mandate to involve these required people. The reply was: 'you are very right to ask this, but we first need to absorb the merger, and then elaborate the strategic goals into a well-oiled organisation. So carry on, you are doing the right thing.' However, the targets were not adjusted for the delay in organisational alignment. As a result, John worked around the clock to get things done. After a while, John started to become tired, and his passion turned into demotivation.

We discussed the broad options:
- Focus on what is good for the business, at the risk of his health (i.e. the current, but unsustainable, path)
- Go with the flow, at the risk of not meeting the targets/the job
- The middle ground: doing the right thing, but adjust to keep alive

John chose the middle-ground. Given that he could not influence his formal mandate, we devised 'the art of the possible':
- Collect an informal set of likeminded people: people who would benefit from his work
- Prioritise a smaller set of customers
- Explicitly work on a business development process (rather than only on chasing everything yourself to score new contracts), that could function across departments: making things easier where cooperation was possible, and devising workarounds where it was not
- Connect with a small number of people in a similar situation for moral support
- Build relationships with (newly, soon to be) powerful people, as a safety net

After half a year, this approach had improved the situation, but not enough. His mood and health did not improve, and the fundamental business model redesign and related organisation was pushed further out. As a result, John started to talk to his HR contact, who understood the issue, and helped John to find another business development role in the same company, a product with much less organisational complexity. John is very happy in this new role.

8.7   The compliance officer

Many years back, Karl worked for a regional government organisation and
was asked to build the compliance processes related to the new European
tendering law. All contracts above a certain amount had to be tendered on a
European scale to promote pan-European competition. Karl diligently studied
the law, and translated it into a solid process manual applicable for his organisation. Then he set about training the various departments how to use the new
rules. Then, nothing happened. Karl started to track new contracts, and found
to his horror that they were still contracted to the well-known suppliers. He
challenged the offenders, who politely apologised, and promised to adhere
to the rules next time. But nothing changed. Karl applied more pressure, but
it did not help. After some time, it became clear that Karl's boss (and above)
wanted to be seen to be early implementers of the new rules, but were afraid
to really enforce them as this would mean requiring various department managers to expend a lot of energy tendering contracts that would often not result
in a better deal anyway.

In hindsight, it would have been better for Karl and his boss to, at least
between them, explicitly agree on the tactics, or game plan, or use a less
ambitious approach.

8.8 The European regional office

Monica had spent 10 years working for a large global IT company, and was in for a change. She found a job in a South American IT company that was fighting their way into Europe. The company was quite successful entering various countries in Europe. The next phase was about building a regional office to harvest the cross-country scale on expertise and multinational clients. Monica was asked to join this European office. She made a plan for how to best create benefits from regional synergies, checked it with her boss, and started to work on this plan. A year later she was suddenly fired, although she had delivered on all the agreed plans. "You should have spent more time on helping the countries on specific needs, rather than working on an overall regional plan". After some digging, it became apparent that the countries did not see the benefit of a stronger regional office, and the management was not willing to risk the successful country entry strategies for the sake of regional synergies.

Monica had noticed the shifting strategy, but she found it hard to challenge the shift in strategy plans as she was in her probation year. She was offended that her performance was suddenly measured against the recent radical new approach. If she had known earlier, she would have adapted her own plans beforehand.

In hindsight: the mandate provider and taker could have both spent a bit more time upfront on internal stakeholder management, and adjusted the plan accordingly.

9   How to use this manual?

People generally don't learn (in the sense of really changing their behaviour) from reading or listening. They learn by trial and error and committing their own experience to their belief system and routines. But sometimes they are looking for ideas to feed their own trial and error. Maybe this manual can serve as that little bit of input. But applying it would be even better. In that case, using this manual is actually very simple.

Below are a few examples of how the manual could be used in four different settings:

- Do it yourself in your own company
- With external help, a mandate sanity check
- In a teaching setting e.g. in an Executive MBA programme
- In a coaching setting

For convenience, the blank check list formats are added at the end.

In a company setting

1. Pick a situation where you are the mandate provider and/or one where you are the mandate taker: you can pick the one that really bothers you or do an easier one first to try it out.
2. Invite your counterpart to participate, and let them read this booklet.
3. Both apply the checklist of the key mandate elements.
4. Compare notes, smile about what you both have missed, and adjust/ mitigate accordingly.
5. Each of you check what reasons you may have for not talking about the mandate, and how you can overcome them. If you both feel comfortable, discuss them. That will create a stronger bond, improving the quality of the next discussion.
6. Think where you may implicitly have provided or accepted a mandate and repeat the above.

Consulting setting: 'mandate sanity check' for both parties

1. Ensure both mandate taker and provider agree to do this
2. Interview the mandate provider and taker individually:
   - On the elements: score the elements and note possible gaps
   - Discuss the barriers to talking about the mandate, ask permission to discuss them
3. Integrate the element list into one, and list the barriers
4. Lead a three-way discussion about:
   - The element scoring/gap list
   - What actions can mitigate these gaps
   - How to operationalise these actions
   - Both barrier lists, and how to avoid this getting in the way during subsequent discussions
5. A small number of elements may need another round to go a step deeper
6. Agree process for subsequent reviews

In an educational setting, e.g. in an executive MBA programme

Duration: Half day plus some preparation work

Preparation work
- Read this manual
- Bring 2 mandate examples:
  - You are the taker of the mandate
  - You are the provider of the mandate

Agenda of the workgroup
- Plenary
  - Brief introduction to the topic (but assume people have read the materials)
  - Brief joint discussion
- Work on your own
  - Apply the checklist of mandate elements
  - List the reasons for the provider and taker not (properly) talking about the mandate
- In small groups
  - Describe each situation to each other
    - From the perspective of the mandate provider and taker
    - What may need to be changed
    - What are you going to do once back at work
  - Jointly select the most interesting example
- Plenary: share the most interesting examples

In a coaching setting (usually with a mandate taker)

A typical coaching conversation with a mandate taker with a not-so-good mandate:

What is the current situation?
- Use the checklist of mandate elements
- What are reasons for the provider/taker not to properly discuss the mandate)

What happens if you don't change anything, the base case?
- Will you achieve the mandate goals, your own goals, is it sustainable/fun/satisfying?

What is your ambition?
- Focus on what is good for the business, at the risk of your health (i.e. the current, but unsustainable, path)
- Go with the flow, at the risk of not meeting the targets/the job
- The middle ground: Doing the right thing, but adjust but keep alive

Elaborate this by asking what is worse than *failing to do the right thing*. It is *succeeding doing the wrong thing*. As you will get respect from people you don't respect, and/or will be asked to do more of the wrong thing. While right /wrong can be in terms of the business or personal goals, mostly it is about doing things that don't really fit with who you really are.

What can you do to improve the situation?
- Adapt/influence the organisation's structure, and people appointments above/around you (usually hard for the mandate taker)
- Ask for a better mandate (mitigations)
- Explicitly review reasons for not (properly) talking about the mandate for yourself, and in a subtle way, for the mandate provider. This could build the main driver: the open relationship between the mandate taker and provider
- Build relationships with (new, soon to be) powerful people, as a safety net

If this is unlikely to be enough, what are the signals to look out for
- Tiredness, bad sleep, de-motivated, irritation, health issues, complaining colleagues

What to do then
- Downsize the objective (inform rather than ask the mandate provider), report sick if you need to

If all else fails
- What is plan B, and at what trigger/event do you start putting mental energy into building/executing plan B

Analysis format

(scale 1-10: 10 is perfect, 8 is great, 6 is just good enough, 3 is bad, 1 is absent)

	Element	Score	Comment
Clear direction			
1	Clear objective & autonomy		
2	Clear strategy/approach		
3	A clear timeline		
4	Alignment with stakeholders		
5	Suitable guardrails		
Suitable mandate provider			
6	Suitable mandate provider		
Well positioned mandate taker			
7	A suitable mandate taker		
8	Suitable reward		
9	Sense of belonging		
Enough Power			
10	Sufficient directly controllable resources		
11	Sufficient power over not directly controllable actors		
Open communication			
12	Open communication between provider & taker		

Reasons for the mandate provider not to talk about the mandate:

Reasons for the mandate taker not to talk about the mandate:

Mitigation format

	Element	Mitigation
Clear direction		
1	Clear objective & autonomy	
2	Clear strategy/approach	
3	A clear timeline	
4	Alignment with stakeholders	
5	Suitable guardrails	
Suitable mandate provider		
6	Suitable mandate provider	
Well positioned mandate taker		
7	A suitable mandate taker	
8	Suitable reward	
9	Sense of belonging	
Enough Power		
10	Sufficient directly controllable resources	
11	Sufficient power over not directly controllable actors	
Open communication		
12	Open communication between provider & taker	
	Other	